21½ STEP MARKETING TRANSFORMATION

Simple, clear and direct Marketing action steps
to get More Sale$ for busy people

Hitul Thobhani MBA

21½ Step Marketing Transformation
Published by Senishi Ltd in 2012

Marketing Sharpness is a brand of Senishi Ltd, Stanmore, Middlesex, UK.
Company number 06831809.

Email: hello@marketingsharpnesstest.com
Website: www.marketingsharpnesstest.com

This book is not intended to provide personalised advice. Readers are encouraged to seek the advice of competent professionals regarding decisions that may impact their business finances or personal wealth. The Author and Publisher specifically disclaim any liability, loss or risk which is incurred as a consequence, directly or indirectly, of the use and application of any of the contents of this work.

ISBN: 9781463737344

Copies are available at special rates for bulk orders. Contact us at hello@marketingsharpnesstest.com.

Praise for the 21½ Step Marketing Transformation and Hitul Thobhani...

"The book is very easy to read and very well written. All the steps are valid and although I knew a lot about what was in the book, it gave me some fresh inspiration. It's good to focus on what can be done for free since costs are one of the prohibitive factors for small businesses. It has given me some food for thought and will help in my marketing planning for the new year."

Candy Jannetta (formerly responsible for marketing for Warner Music and CNN)
Founder and Relationship Coach
How to Meet Your Perfect Match

"I particularly appreciated your notes on writing effective copy, punchy and useful."

Tanya Moore
Founder
The Source of Wellbeing

"Marketing initiates feelings akin to a black hole for me. A never ending list of what you can and should do. If like me you value your time and do not underestimate the importance of marketing, what you are looking for is quick, simple and educated advice based on experience and relevant to your budget. Hitul manages to filter down the chaotic world of marketing into a condensed and systematic format which feels relevant and realistic for you to apply instantly."

Sobia Shah
Co-founder
Cudaboo Ltd.

People who have worked with Hitul Thobhani live have experienced massive breakthroughs. Cémanthe Harries runs New Media Angels, a social media consultancy in London. She was confused and overwhelmed when she arrived at Hitul's seminar. Cémanthe got more from Hitul than a host of other experts at one of the UK's premier business events:

"Wow! Absolutely fantastic workshop and well worth any amount you might pay to attend.

I arrived this morning feeling a bit stressed about how and what to do for my marketing, I'd consulted business advisors and marketing specialists prior to this (as close as yesterday), but none of them made as much sense or gave as much value as Hitul's workshop. His 21 Step process is brilliant and insightful. I can see things to implement straight away to provide instant return. I can't wait to get back to the office to start recommending it to everyone I know! Thanks Hitul!!

Inspiring, thought provoking and all round brilliant!"

Cath Allwood of City Business Library, which is part of the City of London Corporation, provides financial and business information. Cath is not a marketer by background but marketing is part of her job…

"The challenge was to revitalise my writing, which is part of my job. I learned to focus on CUSTOMER – 'you', not 'we'.

Hitul is an excellent presenter, knowledgeable, organised and generous with help and advice. Helped me a lot with rethinking my approach to creating promotional material for CBL."

Elise Saday had recently founded Legal Pragmatics, a specialist consultancy for smoothing transactions for corporate clients, when she attended an event that transformed how she markets her business:

"The Marketing Sharpness event has given me incredible ideas for promoting my business in the right way. Hitul is a very helpful and knowledgeable professional and, no doubt, the marketing strategist that any business should have!"

Gurmit Kaur, founder of Gentle Breathing, got clarity and techniques, but also confidence from Hitul. She needed to sell her audio programmes:

"I was not selling my audio to help people breathe better and my workshop from my website. My business will benefit from converting 'browsers' to buyers by using the techniques Hitul has recommended. Hitul has been really supportive and helpful in identifying words that sell. I now have the confidence to change my website and am amazed at how easy Hitul has made it all."

Vie is a brand of vitamin and health supplements from Global 1st. MD Anuj Shah worked with Hitul to transform his strategy and marketing as part of a three month programme with transformational results:

"Marketing Sharpness has added another dimension to my plans for my newly started business.

Our one-to-one conversations were constructive and valuable.

Hitul has definitely added value to the future of my business with his recommendations which we have taken on board."

For speaking bookings and consultancy contact us at **hello@marketingsharpnesstest.com** or visit **www.marketingsharpnesstest.**

CONTENTS

The 3 phases of the 21½ Step Marketing Transformation

Phase 3
Tactics & Sales Boosters

- *Steps 12 to 21*
- Referral and Marketing Joint Venture strategies
- Testimonials
- Word of Mouth that influences your market
- Use of Video
- Media coverage

Phase 2
Mini Projects - Core Strategies

- *Steps 7 to 11*
- Use 'free' and ease 'know/like/trust' process
- Cash in BIG...after the initial sale
- Build your expert status

Phase 1
Your Marketing Foundations

- *Steps 1 to 6*
- Benefit-led
- Specialising
- Brand and identity
- Position

Introduction

This book is dedicated to transforming your marketing strategy to generate more sales and more profits by making your business Marketing Sharp.

What does a Marketing Sharp business look like?

☑ Learns and applies the secrets from which winning marketers make millions
☑ Markets based on a joined up plan and strategy and is clear and focused about its marketing - not confused or overwhelmed
☑ Generates a strong stream of hot enquiries and motivates enquirers to buy
☑ A website - and all of its marketing – that successfully *sells*
☑ Boosts its sales and profits by being unique
☑ Its customers have a desire and appreciation for its products or services

Do any of these frustrate the heck out of you?

Business owners' frustrations tend to focus on the sales and profit performance of their business. Of the sales and marketing headaches that business owners have shared with me, here are the top 7:

#1. "**Lack of marketing skills** is stopping my business from growing."

#2. "How do I get more **customers and new enquiries**?"

#3. "My **website** and marketing are an **embarrassment** – they are more of a **liability** than a business engine."

#4. "**Competition is savage**. I'm in a constant fight with competitors for business that isn't high margin."

#5. "People are interested but don't **convert into sales**."

#6. "**I hate cold calling** but I need more business."

#7. "I am confused about marketing – **I need a structure and plan!**"

How many of these frustrate the heck out of you?

Is the business you have the business you want? All too often, businesses grow to become a drain on the owner. This book is about re-energising your business and you by Sharpening your Marketing to get the results you want.

This is not an exhaustive text book on marketing. My goal is to make the best possible impact on your business through action steps presented in a punchy, relatable and pragmatic way. Too much detail and depth can get in the way of this.

The 21½ strategies are organised into 3 clear phases to give you a clear structure, starting from the basis of your marketing and strategy and finishing with tactics to boost sales. Hopefully I can help clear any mist you may have around marketing and take away any feelings of overwhelm.

Each step will benefit your business on its own. The more steps you implement, the stronger the results – and the benefits should compound. If you implement the system by doing most or all of the 21½ steps, you can expect much better results as the combined value is much more powerful than isolated tactics.

WEALTH WARNING… *"JUST DO IT"*. Knowledge without action can seriously damage your wealth. Being quick to implement will put you ahead of your slower competitors. You can always change and revise later. Perfectionism rarely pays for business owners. Fast beats slow. Make a call – either you'll be right or learn a lesson.

Experienced business owners: I am guessing you are reading this because there is something you are looking for in your business that it isn't currently delivering. The fact you are reading this suggests you are open to making changes in your business, and appreciate that different results can only come from doing things differently. I applaud your openness to change.

I am one of you, which should hopefully come through as you read. As well as being a marketing specialist, I co-own and co-founded Kidz4Mation, a children's confidence development business. What I am sharing with you in this book is not theory or consultant-speak. The contents of this book come from hard won experience. It takes the best from Marketing Sharpness, my entrepreneurial career, ten years of corporate management and sales and MBA education and condenses it into a clear, brief and practical read with lots of examples.

OK, let's get started. Let's get Sharpening your Marketing.

Here's to your success and profits!

Hitul Thobhani MBA

hello@marketingsharpnesstest.com

Phase 1 – Your Marketing Foundations

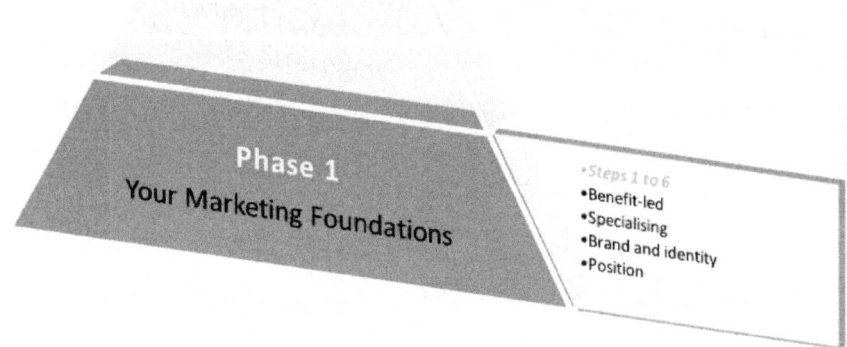

Step 1 - Be customer emotions-led not product led.

Your customer doesn't care about you!

The first trait of a Marketing Sharp business is that is sees itself as solving its customers' problems or meeting their aspirations, and not as the best providers of product X or service Y. I read of a furniture salesman who took pride in selling a comfortable place to sit - not a chair. He probably understands that what he is actually selling is a healthy back, enabling people to enjoy a fuller and more active life (like playing with their children freely or playing tennis again), stress relief and a better place for his customers to entertain their guests.

How does this apply to you? Make sure you define the pain you solve and the value of that to your customer. Ensure you and your team keep this front of mind – so that you don't witter on about yourself and drive business away. Your customers don't care about you or your business – they care about their problems. This is why people come to your business and hand over their money to you. Unless they are friends or relatives, why would they be interested in your business more than any other? In order of importance, your customers care about:

1.   their problem

2.   whether and how well you can solve their problem

3. your products and services

4. your business (second last…)

5. you (in last place!)

Your customers are motivated much more by avoiding pain than achieving gain. Do you know what their worries and fears are in relation to the problem you solve? Understand this and market on it – and the consequences if they choose the wrong product. When someone has a hole in their roof, they look for a roofer and are happy to pay what they ask. The wallet doesn't come out anything like as quickly, if at all, to prevent a leak. The old adage of 'sell the sizzle not the steak' holds a lesson here. Sell on the negative consequences of not buying from you.

I learnt this lesson the hard way with my other business Kidz4Mation. My partners and I saw a vision of changing the world by transforming children's lives. We set out to sell 'personal development for children'…and we struggled! Why? No-one wanted to *buy* personal development for children. So we changed our strategy. We began focusing on what kept parents awake at night. Now that we promote solutions to shyness, lack of confidence, anger and other challenges our customers are much more engaged – because that's what they care about.

A litmus test for your business is to look at how much of your marketing refers to "we", "us" and "our" as opposed to "you" and "your". People don't buy a drill; they buy a 2" hole.

Step 2 - From fierce competition to no competition.

Consider specialising (going niche)

Would you like to end the constant dogfight with your competitors and engage and attract your target market? Sound too good to be true? There is a way: identify a part of the market that you want to dominate and go aggressively after it as a specialist in that niche.

For example, if your business supplies plants to offices, you probably have lots of competitors, who probably source their products from the same supplier as you. So how do you stand out (and price isn't the answer)? First, look at the market and divide it into groups based on customers with things in common (these are called 'segments'). This could be their location (e.g. City of London, West End or Kent), industry, size, or the type of plants (maybe large plants). Then select and focus on one or more of these niches, positioning your company as, for example, the specialist supplier for SMEs based in the City. Your market may now be smaller, but you are in a position to become the 'go-to' company for this market. This is something your competitors will not have. You effectively have no direct competition, and hold a huge advantage over generic competitors who appear to be jacks-of-all-trades by comparison.

People prefer to buy from specialists they feel are best suited to them – and often pay more for the privilege. You can then devote your business to dominating this space. Your brand, its values, your strapline, your website and the look and feel of all your marketing messages should be laser focused to talk loud and clear to your target prospects in tune with their needs. Ensure you do your numbers, understanding the size and profitability of the niche when deciding. This has a major additional benefit online, where you are in a position to rank highly on Google for your niche and will be more likely to engage relevant visitors landing on your site.

Step 3 - Have a clear positioning statement or strapline.

Once you are pain-focused, capture what you do for customers in a few words through your strapline to succinctly convey this so they feel it makes sense to talk to your company. Good straplines often refer to the problem you solve and the uniqueness your company has over competitors in how it solves the pain. They enable your business to create a clear image and place in the prospect's mind. If your company's name isn't familiar to your prospect, it is your strapline that will hook. Remember: people care about their problem.

Think about some of the most famous straplines: "Just do it", "Never knowingly undersold", "Probably the best lager in the world". If you remember them, that shows how effective they are. A good strapline creates a strong and clear brand image in the customer's mind. It defines your business uniquely and sets you apart from competitors. If you don't have one, you need to come up with an effective one that binds with your company's name and its USP.

Step 4 - Get your brand and identity right.

Your brand is your business's personality. It is much more than your logo. It embodies what your business stands for in your customer's eyes. Your goal should be to make your business "sticky" (or magnetic) for your target customers and ultimately make them more likely to spend money with you. This is the job of your branding and identity.

The heart of branding is to think about your business's values and what it stands for – by listing them down – and making sure this comes through in all your marketing: your logo, positioning statement, website, colours, imagery and language. Be consistent – it will help you cement a place in customers' hearts and minds, helping your business become their preferred choice when buying or research a purchase.

Unless you are starting up, you will have a brand and identity. Rebranding is an investment. Any changes might be best phased in, so business generation isn't held up for months while you wait for artwork or new brochures.

Step 5 - Profile your ideal customer.

Once you know which niche you are going for, you need to understand as much as you can about your typical customer. Why is this important? It will allow you to laser in on your target market in a way that is relevant and appealing TO THEM. You want to know the age, family circumstances, income, buying behaviour and typical tastes and preferences of your typical customer. This will allow you to market to them with less wastage in your marketing budget. This applies to the media you advertise in and the messages you convey. For business to business sales, if you haven't already, consider drawing up a hit list of target clients and focusing your efforts on progressing and landing these clients. You can also then look for other non-competing businesses that already have these customers to run marketing promotions with. We will detail this strategy later.

Step 6 - Do you know who your competitors are? Are you sure...?

Have you ever felt overwhelmed by the level of competition for your business or in your product category when you run a search on Google? Your customer could, depending on your business, buy what you sell from companies almost anywhere. Think about who else could solve the same pain for the customer as you. In other words, who else is competing for the same pound or dollar? Thinking about other forms of competition will throw up a different list of names than you traditionally consider competitors. So if you own a book shop, as well as other physical local shops, your competitors are online sellers and also ebook suppliers - and even the growing numbers of online content sources, both paid and unpaid. Then there are providers to mobile and other platforms. This approach is savvy because it is more customer-centred and reflects the buyer's world, their options and thought processes when making a purchase. When you write your marketing copy, you should combat the threat from other forms of competition as well as traditional competitors.

Phase 2 – Mini Projects

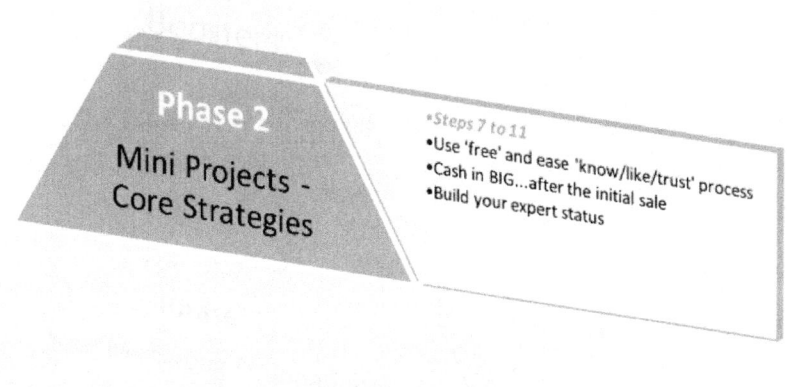

Phase 2
Mini Projects -
Core Strategies

•Steps 7 to 11
•Use 'free' and ease 'know/like/trust' process
•Cash in BIG...after the initial sale
•Build your expert status

Step 7 - Help new customers overcome their fear of dealing with your company.

Focus initially on getting prospects to know, like and trust you.

Every customer you have has been persuaded that they can trust you. They overcame concerns - the fear and uncertainty of buying from a business they haven't traded with before. 'One step marketing', where you say hello in the first sentence and ask for money in the second, is hard work. Marketing Sharp companies know they are much more likely to succeed if they have earned the right to sell.

When customers encounter a new company or website, they are wary of sharing their information and especially handing over money. They ask themselves questions like: "Who is this company? How credible are they? Can I trust them? Can they solve my problem? What will their service be like?" Think about how you would feel if you just discovered a company and were thinking of doing business with them. People are risk averse when they buy. They don't want to make a mistake by misplacing their trust. Armed with this insight, make the first goal of your marketing to not only attract the prospect in the first place but also to overcome their fears. Prove your credentials and win the prospect's trust and they will put their hand in their pocket much more readily. Offering a money back guarantee (or better than money back) if they are not satisfied is a great way of doing this. It shows you are confident in your ability to deliver and takes the risk away from them and onto you. Are you worried that customers will bleed your business dry with requests for refunds? Why would that be in their interests? It just isn't. Don't worry about the cranks. Focus on massive growth; think big. Any refunds will be far outweighed by the extra business your offer wins.

Step 8 - Use 'FREE' cleverly to engage potential customers and have them stick to you.

The word 'free' has magnetism. It is a great hook – people LOVE 'free'. The difference in the impact of free versus 5p or 5c is much more than the money involved. Find or develop something you could offer for free that would be free or cheap for you and valuable to your prospects. Your giveaway will be a stealthy and powerful sales tool. It will build your credibility and show the prospect how wonderful a supplier you would be. There is more on creating valuable content in another step.

If you have a problem with giving things away free, this is probably keeping lots of hot new prospects from you and sending them to your competitors. Any costs you incur should be factored into your cost of sales - make sure it is viable. If you can make a sale on first contact that is wonderful, but you are far more likely to convert that same prospect, and for a bigger sale, after they have grown to know, like and trust you. Amazon and eBay fly in the face of this. They are set up to maximise sales to every visitor. However, they can do this because they have nailed the trust issue, with 90%+ of sales to repeat customers.

Initially, extend your hand, maybe even telling the prospect that you want to win them over so that they become your customer for many years. People don't have a problem with that – try it. Offer something of value on your site and in your advertising. Show them that they should listen to you, trust you and want a relationship with you. Unless you can only make one sale to a customer in their lifetime, their value to you is a multiple of the value of the initial sale. This strategy takes you from being one of many options for your customer to the PREFERRED and trusted choice. A Marketing Sharp business is happy to give a little initially to receive a lot more later. They understand the handsome long term returns and how it helps set them apart from competitors.

Step 9 - Cash in BIG…but AFTER the initial sale.

Marketing Sharp businesses set themselves up to make more money from their customers, the big money, as their relationship with them grows.

Think about the lifetime value of your customer, not the value of the initial sale. Make your initial sale a low commitment one which is easy to say yes to. After you have demonstrated your worth, maybe through a taster of some sort, you are much better placed to sell the main course. Your goal should be to fill your business with a pipeline of customers, a proportion of whom you will make you real money from subsequent higher value sales as you make a difference to them and deliver the results they are looking for. What are the high value services you could offer? One-to-ones, consultancy, premium priced products, a bespoke report, the personal time of you or your senior staff or maybe a premium club or service level. Anything that is personalised and offers unique value to a client can attract a price premium. Whenever you are tailoring to clients' specific requirements, you should cash in.

Once you have done the hard work making the initial sale, don't leave money on the table. The easiest sale is one to an existing customer. It may also be a lucrative one, of higher value than previous sales.

Step 10 - Enhance your expert status.

Don't think you are an expert? If you have been doing what you are doing for a couple of years, you know much more about it than most people. You have specialist knowledge in your area that is valuable to your customers and prospects and are an expert. Experts have credibility. People trust experts. Customers buy more readily from experts and pay more for the privilege.

Here are some great ways to build your expert status and bankability:

1. *Write a book or white paper.* This is a powerful way to build your expert status. Authors have kudos and are perceived as experts. Maybe you don't think of yourself as an author. If you have expertise about your field, which you do if you have at least a couple of years' experience, you have knowledge and insight that would be valuable to others. Authors have gravitas and credibility. In some industries, typically business to business, a white paper that demonstrates your expertise can be very effective. You can then give this away to those who sign up to your list (or make a token charge to cover some or all of your costs). The contents of your brain can be converted into a book much more easily nowadays than before. Freelancing portals[1] allow

you to cheaply source editors and designers and the growth of self-publishing and print on demand means that you don't need a publisher. If you are not comfortable writing, just imagine you are talking about this content with a friend and record yourself. Then, either transcribe it yourself or hire someone through the freelancing portals to do it for you, and get it edited. The printing cost per book should be £1 to £2 (about $1.50-$3.00) depending on quantity. Remember your book is a subtle but very powerful sales tool. Its job is to magnify the customer's problem and portray your business as the ideal solution to it.

2. *Videos,* giving advice and tips, on YouTube or another portal, which you can also upload to your website. Google loves video, so it will boost your ranking!

3. *Post articles* on online article portals.

4. *Podcasts* or *MP3s* – record your comments, analysis, tips or advice using your PC microphone or a digital recorder. Alternatively, get somebody (preferably a friend or colleague) to interview you, but make sure that you control the interview.

5. *Speak at events* – it works wonders for your expert status to be at the front of the room. Get the host to introduce and edify you.

6. *Run seminars* – either free to generate leads or paid to generate revenue and leads.

---

1 There are many, including www.elance.com, www.guru.com and www.peopleperhour.com (which is a British site)

Step 11 - Make £$€000s additional sales by leveraging your expertise.

It never makes sense to leave money on the table. No matter what your field or industry, if you have knowledge that is of value to other people, you are missing out on potentially lucrative extra revenue. You should consider sharing your expertise with clients through selling workshops, training, consulting, speaking, DVDs and audios.

For example, if you are a photographer, you could teach photography and share your expertise through products and services. As well as generating extra revenue, this will enhance your expert status, boosting demand for your core products. If the products replace you, in effect, it might still be worth your while. Weigh it up. Would you have got or been able to service this customer 'live' without the product? Also, the products could fulfill a generic need or a part of the need, with the rest of the problem requiring tailored work from you. One major plus with supplementary products is that they use leverage - you don't need to be there personally. They provide a scalable way to grow your business.

Phase 3 - Tactics and Sales Boosters

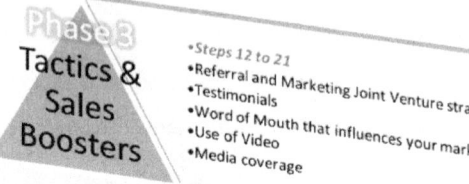

Phase 3

Tactics & Sales Boosters

- Steps 12 to 21
- Referral and Marketing Joint Venture strategies
- Testimonials
- Word of Mouth that influences your market
- Use of Video
- Media coverage

Step 12 - Use at least 7 marketing methods to generate business

Does that sound a lot? If you consider that your website and business card are two of the seven methods, it isn't really. I am amazed at the number of clients who pin all their new business expectations on one or two marketing methods. It takes on average 6 marketing impacts on a prospect to get them to respond.

Here are some but not all of the options available: email marketing (if you're not doing this, you should be!), joint ventures (more about this later), social media, advertising, text marketing, sponsorship, direct mail, public relations, telemarketing, video marketing (via YouTube and other portals), competitions, newsletters, leaflets, posters, speaking, networking and referral.

The magic happens when different methods work together, because the impact they have is compounded. Your odds increase if the prospect receives three messages in close succession. Think about winning mindshare with your prospect. You want to be in front of them with your marketing as often as possible. You won't know WHEN your prospect wants to buy, so if your business is front of mind when they come to buying, you are likely to win their business over a competitor.

Step 13 - The #1 way to grow your business quickly and for free: marketing joint ventures.

Is it possible to have other businesses provide you with lots of new prospects for free? Many of the most successful businesses have grown this way quickly and cost-effectively. It works because it is win-win for both businesses, where both companies help each other to gain new business. There are very few secrets in business nowadays. The prizes go to businesses that join up the dots fastest. Is collaboration the new competition? Maybe. Growing businesses can achieve things by partnering that would otherwise be way beyond them.

How do you go about this? The first thing to do is ask yourself **WHO HAS THE CUSTOMERS YOU WANT**, but doesn't compete with you. For example, if you sell children's furniture, you could partner with a children's clothing manufacturer. You would then promote your offerings to each other's customers, ideally with an exclusive offer or deal. The best response rates are when companies entice each other's customers to provide their contact details in exchange for a free product or information. Surprisingly few businesses use this strategy, yet it is one of the easiest and fastest ways to grow a business. Too many continue to struggle, hoping the customers they crave will come through traditional means, repeating the same marketing year after year. The power of this strategy is that the introduction comes via a trusted relationship rather than a sales call from a stranger. The success rate is much higher than that of cold prospecting, and at a fraction of the cost.

Step 14 - The #2 way to grow your business quickly: a formal referral system.

You probably know how valuable referrals are. But are you capitalising on them fully? Your best salespeople are your current satisfied customers. Potential customers will believe current customers infinitely more than you. Don't take it personally! In fact, as a buyer, you do the same. As a business owner that means you can have other people doing your selling for you. People love to share stories of good suppliers – it makes them feel good about themselves and allows them to help people. Here are some of the ways your business could rake in warm leads that come with a trust factor:

1. *Referral campaigns* – by telesales, email, social media or letter.

2. *Incorporating referral requests into your sales pitch* – especially when the customer is delighted with you.

3. *Incentives* – reward your customers for referring other customers, and reward the people they refer too. Everyone wins!

4. *Measure and track your salespeople on their referral performance.*

Marketing Sharp companies maximise the power of referrals to get lots of new customers in one of the cheapest possible ways. Think of it this way – the alternatives, such as advertising and even pay per click, are likely to be much more costly if you look at the cost of acquiring each new customer.

Step 15 - Maximise the return on your marketing: use permission marketing not spray and pray.

People are flooded with sales messages, most of which they haven't invited. How do you respond to be being stopped in the street or receiving spam email? Marketing Sharp businesses skyrocket their response rates by focusing their efforts on gathering leads then systematically marketing to these people. Think of your marketing and sales as comprising three stages:

1. acquiring new leads with their permission
2. marketing to these leads to make the first sale
3. up- and cross-selling higher value, higher priced offerings

Your response rate is hugely boosted when your prospects have consented to you being in touch with them. How and why would they give you this permission? By accepting your offer of a book, ebook, video or audio in exchange for their email address. The beauty of this is that it gives you access to a list of people/businesses that have some level of interest in and need for what you do. ONCE THEY HAVE REQUESTED INFORMATION FROM YOU THEY ARE IN YOUR TARGET MARKET AND ARE A WARM LEAD. The tip is to provide huge value to your subscribers and weave your selling into this process. Send a combination of training, advice, news, opinion and sales messages and offers. Keep the tone conversational. Do this and you should see a dramatic lift in your response rates and sales.

Step 16 - Get the right people saying good things about your business.

Advertisers pay huge amounts of money to hire celebrities and experts for two main reasons: aspirational value (if you buy our products you can be like this person) but also approval and authority. The approval is a green light from this influential person that this business or product is trustworthy. A paint manufacturer might employ a home makeover show presenter. Food retailers often hire celebrity chefs to inspire shoppers to buy food from them.

For example, a restaurant might say it "offers the finest authentic Thai cuisine in the city". But imagine if that same comment was made by celebrity chef Gordon Ramsay. Doesn't that carry massively more weight? The restaurant benefits from the *credibility* and *trust* of the expert. Trade association badges, awards and professional qualifications also foster trust.

People don't believe what you say about your business until and unless they have a reason to think otherwise. Don't take it personally. As we I said in a previous step, understand you are a stranger to your prospect. When someone they know of and trust says good things about your business, most of the job of persuasion and selling is done. Think about the restaurant example above. This is why PR and media coverage are so powerful and sought after: a credible source (e.g. a newspaper) is saying good things about a business.

Think about who your target market trusts, or the kind of person they would trust. Ask yourself who has rapport with your target market? These are the people who you want saying good things about you. Marketing Sharp businesses find influential experts to say good things about their business without spending thousands for the privilege. Often, a joint venture partner can provide testimony to boost your credibility. Kidz4Mation[2] benefits from endorsements and testimonials from child psychologists, positive psychology academics, teachers and parents.

Step 17 - Testimonials which are believable, specific, relevant and credible.

Most businesses use testimonials, which is powerful for the reason above. You should aim to flood your marketing with testimonials. Customers trust testimonials they feel are genuine. Make your testimonials more believable by giving as much detail about the customer and how you helped them as possible: their full name, business (if applicable) and exact location. How would you respond to a testimonial from "CB, Manchester," versus "Carol Bridge, from Didsbury, Manchester – customer for 4 years"? Isn't the second one far more believable?

Testimonials are most effective and persuasive when they are from a person/business with needs similar to the prospect. Your customer will think, "I can relate to that and I'm looking for something like that." For example, a sports physiotherapist would really persuade prospects with tennis elbow if they presented them with a testimonial from a client whose tennis elbow they

[2] **www.kidz4mation.com**

had successfully treated. This is why you should get testimonials from each type of customer and for each type of need or pain you solve. An accompanying head and shoulders photo of the customer really says 'I am a genuine customer, this company is really good, and you can trust them'. Video is the most powerful form of testimonial; more on that later.

Case studies are longer and more detailed than testimonials. There is a format you can follow for case studies:

1. *The customer's situation and problem before you helped them and why they came to you* – be specific, the more specific the better.

2. *What you did and how you helped* – again, the more specific the better

3. *How wonderful life/business is afterwards* – again, being specific is the clincher. What are the returns/benefits? How much money did they save or make? How much easier/happier did their life become?

Step 18 - Help your customers buy - give them a buyer's guide

Customers have questions and fears when they are buying, as we have already discussed, and they are looking for answers. You can become their best friend in this area by helping them with these, in doing which you put yourself in pole position to get their business.

Suppose you are looking to hire a plumber. You have tens or hundreds of options at your fingertips. Most will claim to be reliable, professional, responsive etc. But how many will help you to choose a plumber? Very few. The plumber that offers a report or page on their website with "7 questions to ask a plumber before you hire them" will put themselves above their competitors. If they help you weed out the bad plumbers and identify the good ones, you are likely to call them.

When you create your report, play to your strengths. The purpose of the report is to paint your business as the perfect choice. This is one of the things that most companies wouldn't do. Do different things to get different results.

Step 19 - Video.

The growth of YouTube and video-enabled smartphones has led more businesses to use video. YouTube is currently the world's #2 search engine; Google is #1 and it owns YouTube. Marketing Sharp businesses use YouTube to boost their search engine rankings. People spend much, much longer online per visit watching videos than reading text. Video is a fantastic way for you to connect with customers and prospects. If you are not using video, you are missing a huge opportunity, one which is powerful and free once it has been created. You can use videos for corporate introductions, tips and advice, interviews, client and expert testimonials and event footage. If you don't want to hire a business video production company, flip cameras - and smartphones - are more affordable in-house alternatives. Both are user friendly and offer good quality footage.

Step 20 - There is a media story in almost EVERY business – find yours and tell it.

Businesses are written about all the time, especially in local media, but also by trade media. You will have read stories about anniversaries, partnerships, big deals, famous clients, competitions, charity/fundraising initiatives and other themes. Media outlets need to fill pages and airtime. A journalist's livelihood depends on finding good stories that are of interest to its audience. Here are some tips on getting PR:

1. *Identify your target media and journalists* – focus, not spray and pray, will pay dividends.

2. *Follow your target media* and look at their previous articles, style, readership etc. Be relevant when you approach – it's their rules.

3. *Be very other-person centred* in handling them – think "what's in it for them?" Find out what their editor has asked them to do a story on and see how your business fits in. Or if you are going to pitch a story, do your homework beforehand. If it has a genuine reader interest, you are much more likely to get a positive response. They are not obliged to write about you, let alone promote you – that is called advertising, which you can control but have to pay for!

4. *It might take time.* Media outlets are flooded with hundreds of calls and emails per day. Journalists are extremely busy and under pressure, so be helpful yet persistent. When you call, ask if they have a couple of minutes to talk – if not call back when they suggest.

5. *Make their life easy* – the less work they have to do to turn what you provide into something they can use, the better your chances.

6. *Be nice!* Build a relationship so you become their 'go to' person.

Step 21 - Test, test, test - and track results so you can ditch what fails

Because you have always done your marketing in a certain way, this does not mean it could not be improved and your returns boosted. Marketing should always be considered an investment, not a cost or overhead. Consider the cost versus the return of all the marketing you do. You might be surprised by the data. This is a good thing, as now you have information you didn't have before, which will help you make even better decisions and get better results than you had got in the past. The tip here is to be open and objective. Don't be subjective or attached to something, especially if it isn't performing. The Yellow Pages don't have a divine right to your money, just because you have always used them.

If you're planning to send out 1,000 emails to your database, you can double or more your response rate by testing first on a small batch. Many businesses play Russian roulette with their marketing budgets by taking a punt with their whole budget rather than backing the winning horse. Don't bet the farm; you don't need to. Find out what works best, then repeat it on a larger scale. By testing, I mean trying different media and experimenting with different variations of, say, a headline, and identifying the top performing one. The key to this is to test one thing at a time; otherwise you won't know the cause of the variation in response rates. Some things can be tested on your timescale, like direct mail, but others require more patience – until say the next edition of a magazine or newspaper. Think learning and improvement with your marketing, not all or nothing one-offs. Keep experimenting and tweaking – you will be surprised by the improvement in your enquiries and sales.

Make media outlets and marketing services providers earn your business. They are desperate for your business and work on huge margins. Be ruthless in the use of your budget.

Step 21½ - Go the extra mile and make a difference to your customers.

"Why this extra half step?" you ask. It is in the spirit of over-delivering. Always give a little bit more than customers expect. It works wonders. Over delivering is a wonderful habit. Doing the bare minimum will, at best, get you by until a competitor sweeps your customers away. Think about how you can delight your customer and make a real and lasting impact on them. Do what you do in such a way that they see you as a partner. Marketing Sharp businesses make themselves hard to replace as a supplier and effectively eliminate their competition by going above and beyond what it says on the tin. They realise it isn't very crowded on the extra mile.

BONUS #1: Meet Your Secret Salesperson

Writing to sell: Here is how to create *killer copy* that persuades and <u>sells</u>!

In business, words are salespeople in print. Whether it is the copy on your website, a marketing email, a sales letter, an advertisement or even your business card, your words (or 'copy') will be ignored unless they capture and keep the reader's attention. Here are some tips on writing to sell:

1. **The headline is the most important part.** This may be surprising as it is the shortest part, but the headline may be 50% of what impacts the reader. Tell yourself that the headline is where you spend most of your money, so to speak. The job of the headline is to stop the reader in their tracks and persuade them to read the introduction. Think about it: it is the clincher as to whether you 'get' the reader. Everything else you write is pointless unless they are captivated by your headline. Focus on your customer's pain and your unique approach to solving it e.g.:

   *"Your **BACK PAIN**...Gone after 3 sessions with ancient herbal Japanese technique. Results Guaranteed!"*

   Come up with different options for headlines and then choose the best from these. I have never got my best, or anything like my best, headline at the first attempt. Expect to work on your headline. See what other people think – ideally someone in your target market. Your headline is too important for you to run with the first thing you think of. Get it right. You'll be glad you spent the time.

2. **Always be customer and benefit led when writing – buyers only think about 'What's In It For Me'.** Remember your goal is to show them you are the right people to solve their problem. If your marketing copy is based on conveying how wonderful your company is, your customer is likely to think "so what?" unless you translate that into a benefit. Customers don't care how long you have been in business; however, they do care that you have hundreds of satisfied customers. Often a feature of your business or product can be translated into a benefit using 'which means' to reveal a compelling benefit. For example, "our product quality is outstanding," has a 'so what?' factor, but when scrutinised with 'which means', might become "we won't let you down or embarrass you." Think about and refer to 'you' and 'your'.

3. **Get your key points in early.** Readers' attention drifts. The further you go in your copy, the more readers you will lose. Before they go, you want to have made your key points (special offer etc.), so try to get them in early and then again at the end.

4. **Structure to sell** - each piece of copy has a different structure depending what it is you're writing, but a general format is. powerful headline, 1st paragraph to summarise, body to support, elaborate and persuade, build credibility and call to action.

5. **Take the reader on a journey.** Linked to having a structure, your text should take the reader from their pain as the starting point to the end, where they make an enquiry, book an event or place an

order with you. The copy should be such that it makes sense to buy from you, and the reader feels that life will be wonderful when they do. Plan your writing with this in mind. Be aware as you write of which stage of the journey the piece is at.

6. **Write emotively.** Buying behaviour is driven by emotions. If you happen to sell industrial machinery or IT systems, you might disagree. However, all copywriters know that as well as persuading the reader, their other challenge is keeping their attention. Copy needs to be engaging to hold the reader's attention, and readers are engaged when their emotions are evoked. The emotions will vary by the type of industry and market a business operates in. Aim to press the emotional buttons of the reader. How can you do this? By touching on their fears, desires, aspirations and values – especially in relation to what you are selling. Emotive prose is persuasive and holds the reader's attention, making them continue to the next paragraph.

7. **Be punchy**. Use short clear sentences - they have more impact. Use short paragraphs also – one per point. Huge blocks of text look daunting, and the reader is likely to stop reading.

8. **Use a conversational tone**. Save the long words - they often get in the way of your sales message. You are not in a writing competition, nor are you trying to impress the reader with your vocabulary. Read what you have written out loud. If it sounds stiff and impersonal, change it - this is how it will come across to the prospect. Write in a way that is personable.

9. **Use numbers and be specific** – numbers catch the eye, stopping the reader when they are scanning. By quantifying, we are being specific. Numbers boost measurability, credibility and believability.

10. **Use powerful quotes from credible sources to persuade and build trust.** Customers believe other customers, especially those who they can relate to, and authority figures in your area of business. For example, a product for babies could be sold well with lots of quotes from mums (and dads), and maybe words of support from the National Childbirth Trust or a celebrity mum with a wholesome public image.

11. **Marketing copy is salesmanship in print.** When you write, you are selling not describing. Getting the enquiry or order will hinge on the effectiveness of your words. It is unlikely that the money will come to you if you simply trot out generalities, facts and features. Good copy can increase your response rates by 100% or even 1000% or more.

Marketing Sharp companies write in a captivating and compelling way with their goal in mind. When you use the 21½ steps and communicate with customers powerfully and persuasively, you'll leave your competitors for dust!

BONUS #2 - Chairman, CEO and Director exclusive: Sharpen your Management

We are on the home straight now! Sharp Marketing can only work in a Sharp business run by Sharp management. We will finish with some pointers on creating a Sharp organisation.

1. **Stop trying to do everything yourself**. Are you running at 100mph? Do you feel your business would collapse if you slowed down? Business owners often have a tendency to feel they have their underpants on the outside, superhero style, and have to ride into town to save the day. Stop chasing your tail, get your time back and get more of your life back. Outsource more and distinguish what to do, what to delegate or outsource and what to ditch. Here are some steps to help you get some sanity and time back:

   a. *How well are you delegating?* If you have a tendency, like a lot of entrepreneurs, to meddle, think about where it will get you. It probably serves a need at some level to feel you have to spread yourself thin and control everything. Ask yourself this...is it going to get you to your goals? If you keep doing what you're doing now, where will your business be in 3 years' time? Don't like the image? Well that's good, because awareness is the start of making the adjustments to your current course. Another way to look at it is that only you can do your job of driving and leading your business and the strategic things that go with that. You can delegate or outsource most other tasks. Don't think anyone could do it quite like you could? You're probably right in many cases. But the people you get to help you will not be able to do the strategic work that only you can do that is essential to move your business forward. Sharp entrepreneurs hire specialists smarter than themselves. Be aware of when you are working IN your business on admin and delivery, and times you are working ON your business. Successful business owners spend at least 20% of their time ON their business rather than getting lost in doing and ending up overwhelmed and exhausted, feeling there are not enough hours in the day.

b. ***Identify the things you and your team can't do.*** Then look at how you can plug these gaps. This may be through freelancers, barters, temporary staff, and permanent staff.

c. ***For the things you can do, consider the time and true cost of doing it in-house.*** Then look at the cost of outsourcing. Think about how much time you would free up and what else could be done when you are working strategically rather than operationally. This is a vital skill for keeping yourself free to steer the ship.

2. **Get it going - don't wait until it's perfect**. Sharp entrepreneurs get it going; fast action normally beats perfectionism and excessive control. Richard Branson's "screw it, let's do it" mentality is about acting boldly, quickly and decisively - rather than fussing over

perfecting a masterpiece. Get it 75% right and get it going - you can always revise later. The returns on getting it perfect don't stack up – the extra few percent of improvement are just not worth it. Become an outstanding implementer and train yourself to get it started rather than getting it perfect.

3. **Buy with time, not money - barter.** Businesses often have goals and needs beyond their means. You might need expertise or consulting you cannot afford, or want some work done that your budget won't stretch to. There is a way to get what you want WITHOUT having to spend money. If you are a printer, you could offer a marketing consultant some free flyers in exchange for a consultation. You don't need to be in a related business to the other company: a chiropractor could barter with an accountant – accountants get bad backs too! Fear of rejection or appearing cheap may worry you. But "he who dares wins," as they say. Bartering allows you to get things you may not otherwise afford, at a much lower price – at the *cost to you* of what you're offering. Make sure you don't forego paid work when bartering.

Summary

So there it is. 21½ clear steps, set out in 3 distinct phases, that when applied, should rock your business and its marketing. In the spirit of the book, I have captured the essence of the 21½ Step Marketing Transformation on one page:

- Be unique and focused, and position your business clearly around your defined specialism. Then aim to dominate and own that territory.

- The worth of your business and its products will be decided by the market. Build your business model around identifying and profitably meeting your customer's needs

- Your new level of clarity should help give more order and structure to your marketing. Aim for your marketing to be linked and aligned.

- Aim to be seen as experts – experts get paid much more than generalists and are harder to substitute.

- Expect to have to win prospects' trust before you get their money. Having engaged the customer with a free or affordable initial offer, cash in with bigger sales, which will be the heart of your business.

- Marketing involves art and science – creativity, planning and analysis.

- Aim to make a difference to your customer and their life/business. Your competitors will not even think about this, which is good for you.

On the journey to Marketing Sharpness your business will develop and you will learn and grow. Good luck. Here's to your success and profits.

Printed in Great Britain
by Amazon

40612113R00030